IF ONLY

IF ONLY

GEORGE MCGOVERN AND THE
AMERICA THAT MIGHT HAVE BEEN

JAMES ARMSTRONG

Library of Congress Control Number: 2014932014

ISBN-13: 978-1494926618
ISBN-10: 149492661X

Cover image by Michael Fisher, background art adapted
from "Starry Night" by Vincent van Gogh (public domain).

Published by PSA Communications
North Berwick ME 03906

≈

CONTENTS

≈

Human Decency

THE PRESIDENTIAL ELECTION of 1972 saw George McGovern buried under an unprecedented avalanche. Richard Nixon had received 520 electoral votes; McGovern only 17. The following morning Henry Steele Commager, one of the 20th century's preeminent historians, entered his Amherst College classroom and said, "It's a sad day for me. It's a sad day for America. Because we have just missed an opportunity to elect a modern day Thomas Jefferson."

Later McGovern would say, "I have to live with the knowledge that, not only did I lose the election, but I lost it to the most discredited man ever to occupy the White House." If only the outcome had been different … .

"If onlys" clutter the pages of American history.

If only George Washington had agreed to become a king instead of a president; if only Abraham Lincoln had lived to preside over the reconstruction of a battered, reeling nation following the Civil War; if only John F. Kennedy, Martin Luther King, Jr. and Robert Kennedy had not been shot down in the '60s; if only George McGovern had been elected President of the United States in 1972 – how different the story of our land would read.

On the 25th anniversary of Watergate, Al Neuharth, founder of *USA Today*, asked, "What if Watergate had elected McGovern?" Among other things he said:

- Nixon would have gone down in history as just another one-term president, without disgrace and with generally pretty good marks.
- The Vietnam War would have ended more than three years sooner.
- The Cold War would have ended in the '70s rather than in the '90s.

Neuharth wrote, "In a real sense George McGovern was the main victim of Watergate. He saw it for what it was – the tip of an iceberg in a wicked White House."

He went on, "McGovern was a man before his time. Prescient. Decisive but decent. The USA would have been far better off if we had been heedful of his early Watergate warnings and had put McGovern in the White House in 1972."

Andrew Cohen was a 17-year old youth when he joined "McGovern's Army" in '72. He called it "an eager band of students, idealists, naifs, reformers, potheads and peaceniks." Now, nearly half a century later, Cohen is a professor of journalism and international affairs at Carleton University, Canada's "capitol university". In retrospect he calls the McGovern campaign "a beautiful failure." He writes, "Whatever his loss, George McGovern was no loser. He was a patriot of the highest order – principled, gutsy, progressive, independent. He was right then and right now." Gary Hart called his book about the campaign, *Right from the Start.*

Why write about George McGovern now? He breathed his last on October 12, 2012, at 90 years of age. He's gone. But is he? True, he's buried in a Washington, D.C. cemetery. But, is he really dead and gone? Maybe, if some of us revisit him, we can bring essential parts of his reality back to life.

I knew George and Eleanor McGovern for half of our lifetimes. We first met as United Methodist delegates to the General Assembly of the World Council of Churches in Uppsala, Sweden, in 1968. A few months later I was elected to the United Methodist episcopacy. As a bishop, I was assigned to preside over the church's affairs in North and South Dakota. I became the McGovern's bishop. They attended my installation in Aberdeen, and he dictated a routine letter the following day suggesting that he and Eleanor looked "forward to many pleasant associations with (me) in the years ahead." Little did we know.

The following pages will detail McGovern's prairie roots and value system, his patriotism and heroism in World War II, his lifelong love affair with his "Dakota Queen" (he named his World War II B-24 bomber after his wife, Eleanor), the evolution of his career path from pilot to parson to professor to politician, his unmatched record in providing food for the world's hungry, his years in the U.S. Senate, and his legacy.

DURING HIS YEARS in Washington I was stationed in the Dakotas and in Indiana. However, I chaired two of my denomination's justice and peace agencies headquartered in Washington. The McGovern home in Washington became my home away from home. Our daughter, Becky, served on his staff. I, joined by Father Robert Drinan, Dean of the Boston College Law School and later, a Congressman (the first to call for the impeachment of Richard Nixon), officiated at

4

Becky's wedding held in the McGovern home. Over the years ours became a profoundly meaningful, intimate friendship.

One memory, among a host of others, stands out in my mind. It was the day Richard Nixon would resign as America's president. Life in Washington had come to a standstill. The McGoverns were scheduled to attend a dinner at the French Embassy, but the dinner was cancelled. The Senator called and asked if I would join their family in listening to Nixon address the nation. As we sat in their family room looking at the TV set, with the McGovern youngsters draped over the furniture and sprawled on the floor, the President spoke. The criminality of Watergate and the humiliation of the crushing presidential defeat were fresh in mind. The younger McGoverns began to fill the air with noisy merriment until their father, calmly but firmly, told them to quiet down. He reminded them that not one of us could comprehend the anguish the president was experiencing at that moment. The fundamental decency of a remarkable human being was quietly revealed. No wonder Bobby Kennedy called George McGovern "the most decent man in the Senate," adding wryly, "As a matter of fact, he's the only one."

In 1998, Tom Brokaw described those he considered members of the "Greatest Generation." He included McGovern, writing, "He remains one of the country's most decent and thoughtful public servants." That word, "decent," keeps cropping up.

≈

The Seedbed of Values

DECENCY, HUMAN DECENCY – where did such integrity come from? Who can fully understand the vagaries of personality development; the roots of one's character and value system?

The *New York Post* once editorialized: "George McGovern did not go out and buy his decency, he did not hire Young and Rubicam to spray him with tinsel and lacquer. He did not sit down and calculate his image. He earned it! His decency was formed by the facts of his life, by the experience of the poverty and hunger in the depression dust bowls around Avon, South Dakota where he was born, by growing up among bone-sore farmers in the prairie town of South Dakota."

Looking at George McGovern it can be assumed that some of it came from the piety of his Wesleyan Methodist parsonage heritage on the Great Plains. It came from his wartime experience as he witnessed the cruel deaths of friends. It came from his education in a small private college in South Dakota, a theological seminary, and in Northwestern University's graduate school. It came from his reading the social gospel of Walter Rauschenbusch, and from listening to the brilliant, relevant sermons of Harry Emerson Fosdick and Ernest Fremont Tittle. It came from observing poverty and desperate need during his boyhood years of the Great Depression, and from his travels across the Third World where he saw widespread malnutrition and corruption as he directed the Kennedy administration's Food for Peace program. And, it most assuredly came from interacting with his beloved life-long partner, Eleanor, who died in January, 2007.

In an article written in 1971 (*The Christian Ministry*, July 1971), he paid tribute to his father, Rev. Joseph C. McGovern. As he described his father serving congregations and building churches across his state he wrote, "Through it all, as I grew in awareness, I watched my father with people. I watched him care for and care about the people who were struggling with the land and with the Depression that turned South Dakota into a tragic, hunger-ridden dustbowl. But through it all no one gave up. The commitment that my father had and fostered in the people who gathered around him is what kept them going." *The commitment my father had and fostered in those who gathered around him –* like father like son; a more than worthy heritage.

Rev. Joseph McGovern and my grandfather, Rev. Fred Armstrong, were cut from the same piece of cloth. At the turn of the century Grandad Armstrong left a farming community in southern Michigan to go, as a missionary preacher, to the western reaches of the Great Plains - Montana. In 1910, he wrote an article for the *Montana Christian Advocate,* urging his readers to embrace the Wesleyan doctrine of "holiness of heart and life." He condemned smoking, drinking, dancing, card playing, gambling, and theater-going. He detailed the moral standards of Wesleyan Methodism, standards that would later, in a somewhat modified form, be imposed on young George McGovern. George was obedient to a point, but confessed that he often sneaked out to go to a movie theater. He was a good kid, but not *that* good.

The value system of the Upper Plains was stern and demanding, but the climate was harsh, the soil was dry and barren, and the struggling people were not that far removed from the pioneer stock that had settled the region.

George McGovern was born in 1922, in Avon, South Dakota, a farming town inhabited by about 600 dirt-poor souls. His father was the Wesleyan Methodist pastor there. When George was only three years old the McGoverns moved to Calgary, returning to the United States, and to Mitchell, South Dakota, three years later. In 1927, Charles Lindbergh made his transatlantic solo flight and became little George's hero.

As a boy McGovern was painfully shy. He attended the public elementary school where he was advanced "conditionally" from the first to the second grade because of that shyness. His family lived on the frayed edges of poverty. His father was never paid more than $100. a month, and, as often as not, was paid with potatoes, cabbages or a slab of beef.

When George was in high school his life took a dramatic turn when he was recruited for the debate team. As a debater he learned to study hard, to research subjects that were foreign to him, to think on his feet and to forcefully express himself. Graduating near the top of his class, in a state passionate about the art of debating, he had become a star.

McGovern's debating skills earned him a scholarship to Dakota Wesleyan University in Mitchell where he was elected class president during his sophomore and junior years. In 1942 he won South Dakota Peace Oratory Contest. His theme? "My Brother's Keeper" - a reminder that we are here to serve the needs of those about us, especially those who are weak and helpless. It was later recognized as one of the twelve best speeches delivered in the United States that year by the National Council of Churches and was circulated nationwide by that body.

In February, 1943, young McGovern and his partner won a national debate contest that featured participants from over one hundred schools. He would later say, "Debate was the one thing I could do well. It really became the only instrument of personal and social power I had. Indeed, my own life was transformed by the efforts to persuade others." Actually, "transformed" was literally true.

Eleanor Stegeberg was born in 1921 in her grandfather's farm house near Woonsocket, South Dakota. She came into this world just thirty seconds after Ila, her twin sister, appeared on the scene. They grew up together, went to school together, were cheerleaders for tiny Woonsocket High School, and were partners on the school's debate team. Unlikely as it seems, she and her sister defeated McGovern and his partner in a statewide debate tournament.

That did it. The die was cast. Life for George McGovern and Eleanor Stegeberg would never be the same.

≈

Eleanor and Patriotism

GEORGE AND ELEANOR soon became an "item" on the Dakota Wesleyan campus. They went to movies together, to the skating rink, to the corner drug store for cokes, to DWU's chapel services. They wandered over the campus hand in hand, sharing their ideas and dreams. Finally, George took her home to meet his parents. In the fall of 1941, they began making plans for a life together. But, there were other considerations.

George's seventh grade gym teacher called him a "physical coward" because he seemed unable to perform some required gymnastic contortions.

Realizing that there might be a measure if truth in the comment he began to muscle up. In high school he made the track team. He took flying lessons, confessing that flying "scares me silly," and earned his pilot's license. After completing his first solo flight he emerged from the cockpit drained and weak-kneed, but triumphant. He was confronting his demons and preparing himself for the future.

On Halloween in October of 1943, George McGovern and Eleanor Stegeberg were married in the little Woonsocket Methodist church. George's father tied the knot.

Suddenly the world changed for George and Eleanor as it changed for every American. Japan's bombing of Pearl Harbor on December 7, 1941, was beamed across the airwaves as George was working on his college music appreciation assignment and listening to a broadcast of the New York Philharmonic orchestra. He was nineteen, he had his pilot's license, and there was a cause to be served and a war to be fought. He was nineteen and he volunteered.

McGovern was sworn in as a private at Ft. Snelling, Minnesota. There followed a period of intensive training that took him from Jefferson Barracks in Missouri, to Carbondale, Illinois, to Texas and Oklahoma and Kansas. Finally he was assigned to a transition school to learn to fly the B-24 Liberator bomber. He described his training as "the toughest (he) ever experienced." The B-24 was a bulky monster. "If you can imagine driving a Mack truck without any power steering or power brakes, that's about what it was like at the controls," wrote McGovern.

After their marriage Eleanor went with him from post to post and was present when he was given his wings and commissioned a second lieutenant.

Lt. McGovern was assigned to the 741st Squadron of the 455th Bombardment Group of the Fifteenth Air Force, stationed in the Apulia region of Italy. From there he would fly 35 missions (the maximum allowed) over enemy territory, hitting everything from oil refineries to railroad yards to (by mistake) an isolated farm house in Austria. He was haunted by the knowledge of that accident until, forty years later, he was visiting Austria and the farmer learned of his presence in his country. The farmer told the media that no one had been hurt, and that the scare had been altogether worth it in a war to destroy Adolf Hitler. You can imagine the former bomber pilot's relief.

IT IS HARD TO IMAGINE what it was like to fly those lumbering box-cars into the thundering fury of air warfare. One day a piece of shrapnel from flak shattered McGovern's windshield narrowly missing him. Another time his co-pilot, a close friend, was killed by shrapnel as he sat by McGovern's side. He once landed *The Dakota Queen* with 110 holes in her. B-24s were always endangered species on their take-offs. When their wheels were blown they often crashed and their crews were killed. One day McGovern's wheel was blown, but he managed to take off, complete his mission over Germany, and return without further damage.

On a mission over the Skoda works in Czechoslovakia, McGovern's plane was hit by flak, one engine was killed and another was on fire. Unable to return to Italy, he flew to a tiny British-controlled island in the Adriatic Sea and successfully landed on a frighteningly short airstrip. For that feat, at the age of 22, he was awarded the Distinguished Flying Cross.

In 2007, in a speech delivered in Chicago, former Vice-President Dick Cheney called George McGovern's patriotism into question. Writing in the *Los Angeles Times,* McGovern responded:

"In the war of my youth, World War II, I volunteered for military service at the age of nineteen and flew 35 combat missions, winning the Distinguished Flying Cross as the pilot of a B-24 bomber. By contrast, in the war of his youth, the Vietnam War, Cheney got five deferments and has never seen a day of combat – a record matched by President Bush."

The self-congratulatory note was uncharacteristic, but altogether called for. McGovern's debating skills had been finely honed.

Stephen Ambrose, a Pulitzer Prize winning historian and author of more than 30 books, wrote *The Wild Blue,* the story of George McGovern and his crew, of "the men and boys who flew the B-24s over Germany 1944-45." Among many other things it describes McGovern's qualities of loyalty and leadership that would have served the nation so well … if only.

Calling McGovern "one of the greatest patriots I know," Ambrose rightly insisted that "You don't necessarily have to be a hawk to be a patriot."

Robert Novak, a conservative nabob, after reading *The Wild Blue,* said, "I can never think of George McGovern again in the same way. Of course he was a genuine hero. He was a great leader."

Senator McGovern first came to national attention as a strident, vocal opponent of the Vietnam War. He did not endear himself to many of his colleagues when, in responding to an onslaught by Senator Everett Dirkson of Illinois, he responded, "It doesn't require any particular bravery to stand on the floor of the Senate and urge our boys to fight harder, and if this war mushrooms into a major conflict and a

17

hundred thousand young Americans are killed, it won't be U.S. Senators who die. It will be American soldiers who are too young to qualify for the Senate." (Anson, p. 160)   During a Senate floor debate in 1970, he charged, "Every Senator in this chamber is partly responsible for sending 50,000 young Americans to an early grave....This chamber reeks of blood....it does not take any courage at all for a Congressman or a Senator or a President to wrap himself in the flag and say we are staying in Vietnam, because it is not our blood that is being shed." He blamed his colleagues for "the human wreckage all across our land – young men without legs or arms or genitals or faces – or hopes" (*Time*, 1972).

Predictably, such angry rhetoric was met with equally angry responses. McGovern was called a spineless peacenik, an unrealistic dreamer, unpatriotic, un-American. Paying editorial tribute to the one-time Senator in 1995, the *Christian Science Monitor* said:

"What Mr. McGovern is telling the president is that he should stick to his Principles – and let the chips fall where they may. McGovern surely did that, standing up to angry criticism of his position against the Vietnam War. He was drubbed by the voters, but he's been vindicated by history."

McGovern once wrote, "To remain silent in the face of policies that one believes to be hurting the nation is not patriotism, it is cowardice. ... Criticism of public policy does not weaken the nation; rather it serves to refine, correct or strengthen our national course" (*Response,* 1971). It was Albert Camus in one of his *Letters to a German Friend,* who wrote, "This is what separated us from you: we made demands. You were satisfied to serve the power of your nation and we dreamed of giving ours her truth..."

Martin Niemoeller was being patriotic when he cried from his pulpit, as members of the Gestapo listened, "*God* is my Fuhrer."

Nelson Mandela spent a quarter of a century in South African prisons because, as a patriot, he fought against *apartheid.*

Martin Luther King, Jr., was threatened, brutalized, and imprisoned time and time again because, as a strong-willed patriot, he challenged racial segregation when it was the law of his region. Writing from a prison cell he addressed some of his critics. "Let us all hope," he wrote, "that the dark clouds of racial prejudice will soon pass away and that the deep fog of misunderstanding will be lifted from our fear-drenched communities and in some not too distant tomorrow the radiant stars of love and brotherhood will shine over our great nation with all their scintillating beauty" ("Letter from Birmingham Jail").

Speaking before the Washington, D.C. Press Club in 1991, George McGovern referred to Lee Atwater, the Republican national chairman who had been stricken with cancer. Atwater had told *Life* magazine, "My illness helped me to see what was missing in society was missing in me: a little heart, a lot of brotherhood. The '80s were about acquiring – acquiring wealth, power and prestige...I don't know who will lead us through the '90s, but they must be made to speak to the spiritual vacuum at the heart of American society." McGovern closed his remarks with these heartfelt words: "I am proud of the things for which I have stood, the battles I have fought – and am determined now, in every way I can, to muster the courage to stand for my beliefs" (*Nation Building*, 1991). McGovern helped fill a number of vacuums in American life. He had joined Oliver Wendell Holmes as a "great dissenter."

McGovern insisted that patriotism is the capacity to be self-critical, to call one's own nation to judgment, to be *dissensual*; nor does patriotism belong to one school of thought, one ideology, or one political party.

For the past decade our nation has been sharply divided; Washington has been riddled through with strife; Congress, with its lowest favorability ratings ever, has been obstructionist – literally, a "do nothing" Congress. Gone are the days of moderation. There is a question as to whether the present-day GOP would even welcome Theodore Roosevelt, Charles Evans Hughes, Jacob Javits, Nelson Rockefeller, Dwight Eisenhower, or even Ronald Reagan, into its ranks. President Obama's efforts to cross the aisle and be bipartisan have been repeatedly thwarted. The aisle has grown too wide. Writing for *The Nation* in 2005 (April 11, 2005), George McGovern wrote an opinion piece called, "Patriotism is Nonpartisan."

He numbered among his friends Republican colleagues like Barry Goldwater, Mark Hatfield, George Aiken, Jacob Javits, and Richard Lugar. He admired President Eisenhower and claimed that his approach to foreign policy was patterned after that of the former Republican president who warned against the domination of a "military industrial complex" as he left office. McGovern called Republican presidential candidate, Bob Dole, a "true compassionate conservative" and a "national treasure" (the same Bob Dole who, not too long ago, said that the present GOP should hang a sign on its door saying, "Closed for Repairs").

In his article on the non-partisanship of patriotism, McGovern wrote:

"As the son of a Wesleyan Methodist clergyman, I dare say my life has always been enriched by the Judeo-Christian ethic. Nothing has influenced my philosophy more than the Hebrew prophets and the Sermon on the Mount."

He concluded with a poignant memory:

"Recently the officers and enlisted personnel of Ellsworth Air Force Base in Rapid City, South Dakota, in the magnificent Black Hills under the shadow of Mount Rushmore, named a B-1 bomber 'The Dakota Queen' – the name of the B-24 bomber I flew in World War II, so titled in recognition of my wife, Eleanor. After a moving ceremony attended by Eleanor and me, one of the junior officers said to me, 'Senator, I don't know if it bothers you to be called a left-wing liberal, but just remember that a plane can't fly without both a left wing and a right wing!' That's the kind of common sense that prompts my admiration and to which I say Amen and God bless us all – even those of us who are unmarried or have deeper love for one of their own sex than of the opposite sex. In the Methodist parsonage where I was reared we were taught that we should always be cautious about judging one another. Such judgments are more properly left to the Almighty rather than to the political hustings and the quest for partisan advantage."

Patriotism is non-partisan. So is morality.

≈

Society and the History Prof

MCGOVERN RETURNED from the war in Europe to resume his studies at Dakota Wesleyan. Majoring in history and government he graduated magna cum laude in 1946. What would follow?

George's boyhood home was deeply religious. Every day began with family devotions.. Speaking to the students of Wheaton College in 1972, he explained, "Daily teaching from the Scripture, and a constant immersion in faith, made an indelible imprint on me." His sobering wartime experiences, coupled with his stern religious origins, led him in predictable directions. He would follow in his father's footsteps and become a minister.The young McGovern family moved to northern Illinois where George would attend Garrett Biblical Institute and serve the little Diamond Lake Community (Methodist) Church as a "student supply."

After a year he realized that he and the ministry were not meant for each other. Northwestern University was adjacent to Garrett. He crossed over, entered Northwestern, earned his Master's degree, and began working on a Ph.D. in history.

The years at the university were years of threadbare hardship. Later Eleanor would recall: "Sometimes we subsisted for weeks on peanut butter, soup and milk, budgeted out of an unreliable income made up of George's G.I. veteran's check, money he earned tutoring student athletes, extra cash I contributed by sitting in a closet to type masters' theses and doctoral dissertations, plus a few pennies George collected by turning in empty soda bottles scrounged around the apartment house."

In 1950, while still working on his dissertation, he returned to Dakota Wesleyan to teach history and coach the debate team. At the time of McGovern's death a former student (Dorothy Schwieder), who later taught history at Iowa State, remembered those days:

"He influenced the lives of so many when he was there. He did such a fine job in the classroom." Realizing that the tributes being paid McGovern were related to his later years as a statesman senator, she said, " I just thought I had to get something down about *that.*"

Another writer (Nancy Grund), describing his return to teaching after his retirement from public life, spoke of his "natural rapport" with students, he seemed "perfectly at ease fielding questions from the class on topics as diverse as the Radical Right and Salt II."

I can vouch for that.

A few years ago McGovern was visiting us. At the time I was teaching a course on "ethics and political realism" at Rollins College. I asked him to come with me and meet with the class. He acquiesced; nothing seemed more natural. He sat on the edge of my desk, and, with a lanky leg dangling, he respectfully listened to students' questions, responded with great care, and interacted with them in ways they will never forget.

He returned to Dakota Wesleyan from Northwestern, using DWU, as Peter Harriman put it, "as a parking place while he completed his dissertation." Complete it he did, writing a 450-page description of "The Colorado Coal Strike, 1913-1914."

True to form, McGovern sided with the miners as they rebelled against Rockefeller interests in the coalfield war. His faculty advisor at the time, the noted historian Arthur Link, said he had never had a better student in all his years of teaching.

In 1953, against the advice of his friends, he left his teaching position to become executive secretary of the South Dakota Democratic Party. That may sound grandiose, but no Democrat held a statewide office and Democrats held only 2 of 110 seats in the state legislature. He and Eleanor crisscrossed the state in their rickety car, writing down names, addresses and personal data related to virtually everyone they interviewed; a data bank that would later prove invaluable. They kept the fruits of their labors in a shoebox. Later George would say, "It is no small task to write a longhand description of every person one meets. No computer can ever duplicate the human feeling I gave to that old shoebox." In 1954, Democrats won 25 seats in the legislature. In 1956, McGovern ran for Congress and was elected.

During this season of his life McGovern's political interest moved far beyond the borders of his remote prairie state. In 1948, he was drawn to the presidential candidacy of Henry Wallace and attended Wallace's Progressive Party's national convention. Later, believing that the Party had been unduly influenced by communist "crazies," he supported Harry Truman. In 1952, he heard Adlai Stevenson's speech accepting the Democratic presidential nomination. Profoundly moved, he wrote a number of supportive articles for Mitchell's newspaper, the *Daily Republic*. He and Eleanor named their newborn son, Steven.

From his earliest days as a student, through his professorial career and his years as a public servant, McGovern immersed himself in history, global affairs and political science. While "relaxing" during a wartime R-and-R break, the B-24 bomber pilot went to Rome, basked in the glories of the past, had an audience with the Pope, and read Charles and Mary Beard's classic, *The Rise of American Civilization*. In his autobiography (*Grassroots*) he would write, "The Beards attempted to reach beyond the traditional historical account of political, military and diplomatic events to achieve an understanding of all the complex forces that shape a developing society." He then quoted Voltaire who had written, "I wish to write a history, not of wars, but of society."

Hans Morgenthau and Reinhold Niebuhr were two of America's most prominent political ethicists of the twentieth century. Morgenthau outlined "six principles of political realism" starting with an insistence that "politics...is governed by objective laws that have their roots in human nature."

Niebuhr listed five recurring themes in his

understanding of political realism:

- an explicit nature of man;
- a distrust of moral perfectability;
- the importance of history;
- avoid moral absolutes; and,
- the inescapable role of power politics.

McGovern would have agreed with both scholars as they spoke of the importance of history and the inescapable reality of power politics. However, he had a far more positive and hopeful view of human nature than either Niebuhr or Morgenthau. He would have agreed with Carl Rogers' concerning the human potential.

CARL ROGERS WAS AMERICA'S most influential psychologist in the twentieth century. I was privileged to study with him at the University of Chicago's Counseling Center. It is probable that McGovern had only a vague awareness of his thought. Yet the two, as they dealt with the human condition, had much in common. They both envisioned a better world than the one we now inhabit. They both devoted their energies and resources to the development of that "better world." Rogers wrote about the "world of tomorrow" being shaped by "the person of tomorrow." Realizing how rapidly and radically the world was changing Rogers described that person:

- The person would be open, open to new ways of seeing, new ways of being, new ideas and concepts.
- The person would desire authenticity, not be two-faced and hypocritical, but real.
- The person would be skeptical regarding science and technology. Life can't be reduced to quantitative measurements. We are persons with minds and spirits.
- The person would desire wholeness, "with thought, feeling, physical energy, psychic energy, healing energy all being integrated into experience" (Rogers, *A Way of Being*).
- The person would wish for intimacy, for new forms of communication, verbal as well as non-verbal, feelingful as well as intellectual.
- The person would be a process person, willing to take risks; vitally alive in the face of change.
- The person would be caring, gentle and non-judgmental.
- The person would have a positive attitude toward nature, seeking to conserve its beauty and energy rather than exploit its resources.
- The person would be anti-institutional, believing that institutions should exist for people, not the reverse.

- Persons would find their authority within, making their own moral judgments.
- Persons would recognize the unimportance of material things. This is a toughy, but we tarnish our selfhood if money and material status symbols become our goals.
- And finally, persons would have a yearning for the spiritual. They would recognize the power and beauty reflected in the lives of Mahatma Gandhi, Mother Teresa, Martin Luther King, Jr. and other humanitarian activists. They would long to experience the unity and harmony of the universe; to become self-transcendent. People like these would change the direction of human history.

Carl Rogers and George McGovern, a psychologist and a politician, experiencing and defining persons and history, the ingredients of the human story. Is it overreach to try to bring the many facets of our social landscape together? Not if you believe what Voltaire, the Beards and George McGovern had to say about history being more than a description of wars and governments and laws. It is the story of society; of people like you and me who give society its shape and direction.

≈

One Man's Family

IN 2002, I WROTE a personal memoir, *Feet of Clay on Solid Ground.* In it I confessed:

"As a father I was not as available as our youngsters deserved and needed me to be. As a husband I was not as thoughtful and attentive as I should have been. My speaking engagements, early morning study habits, outside commitments, civic involvements, and willingness to respond to every Tom, Dick and Mary coming down the pike negated the possibility of a stable, balanced, healthy home life."

I sent a copy of the book to McGovern. His thank-you note acknowledged that I had described him with deadly accuracy.

His years on Capitol Hill gave him little choice. During the late 1950s Lyndon Johnson was the Senate Majority Leader and Sam Rayburn was Speaker of the House. McGovern explained, "Rayburn was a bachelor and Johnson was immersed in politics. They had no sympathy for a congressman who couldn't work 15 or 18 hours a day." As one observer (Seth Tupper of *The Daily Republic*) noted, "The long hours took a toll on his family life."

During the late '60s and '70s I was in and out of the McGovern home countless times. The younger McGoverns were coming and going. Eleanor was homemaking, shopping, seeing her doctors (even then she had health problems) and hostessing. Sometimes things were calm and quiet. More often than not they bordered on hectic. It all depended on the Senator's schedule.

For obvious reasons, during the early years of their marriage things were much calmer. Eleanor joined George as he moved from post to post as an Air Force trainee. They were as close as peas in a pod during his years at Northwestern and when they returned to Dakota Wesleyan. They were side by side when they singlehandedly resurrected South Dakota's Democratic Party.

When Eleanor died in 2007, the Madison (Wisconsin) *Capitol Times* mentioned the fact that on the night of the Wisconsin primary in 1972, McGovern had referred to Eleanor as his "most devoted campaigner." The *Capitol Times* continued, "He was more than recognizing a loved one...he was stating a fact." It went on, "She threw caution to the wind. She hit the trail on her own, going to towns her husband could not reach, writing and delivering her own speeches and holding her own with the press. She was the first wife of a presidential candidate to make a solo appearance on NBC-TV's "Meet the Press," answering policy questions without hesitation and in precise detail." George and Eleanor McGovern were a team.

On their 60th anniversary they renewed their vows in an historic old chapel just off the DWU campus. About 60 people, mostly students, had gathered there. At the time the McGoverns had four surviving children, ten grandchildren, and six great-grandchildren. Steve, their only son, later died in a rehab center at the age of 60. He was an alcoholic.

Terry had died at the age of 45 in 1994. She began drinking with school friends when only 13. She became pregnant the first time she had sex at the age of 15, had an abortion, and was haunted by that fact for the rest of her life. At 19, when her father was running for president, a Republican orchestrated arrest led to her incarceration in Rapid City, South Dakota, for smoking pot. McGovern, who was campaigning in California, suspended his campaign and flew to Rapid City to be by her side. Terry was hospitalized for depression, slipped unseen out of the hospital, and attempted suicide.

Terry was a lovely, intelligent, fragile young woman. She and her father had a special, humor-laced, relationship. But, she had become an alcoholic, a genetic vulnerability that seemed to run in the family. George McGovern's grandfather, his brother Lawrence and his son Steve, fell victim to it.

For eight years, during her thirties, Terry was "dry." She had given birth to three lovely children, but something snapped. She fell off the wagon with a resounding thud. Her father footed the bills as she was moved in and out of a succession of rehabilitation centers. On the night of December 13, 1995, Terry left her detox center in Madison, Wisconsin, and went to a bar where she downed shot after shot of vodka. About midnight she stumbled out into the freezing air, collapsed in a snow bank, and froze to death.

George's book, *Terry,* spoke in agonizing detail about Terry's life of hope and promise, her addiction, her struggle, her death, and the continuing challenges we face as we deal with the ravages of addictive thought and behavior. Matthew Rothschild, editor of

The Progressive, called *Terry* "the saddest book I ever read." McGovern hoped that his portrayal of Terry would help others who were trying to cope.

AT THE TIME OF TERRY'S DEATH, I wrote to the McGoverns:

"You know, far better than I, how bright and good Terry was, and how she longed to be rid of her inner demons. On two occasions – once by phone and once at one of those expensive rehab centers you made possible for her – we talked about the human will and spirit, inner resources and feelings of utter helplessness. We talked about addiction, disease and the illusiveness of 'cure.' How I wish I could have been more helpful.

"If you are human (and you are) you are thinking of things you might have done differently. In retrospect there is always a flood of 'if onlys.' But, dear friends, given the unusual circumstances of your lives you did what you could, made yourselves available again and again, and invested immeasurable emotional/spiritual energy in Terry. Only she could function for herself – and she did."

In the election of 1980, a number of liberal senators were defeated by New Right, "family values," Republican candidates. McGovern was one of those who fell. He was trounced by a gentleman named James Abnor. Commenting on his defeat he smiled and said, "It ticked me off, and it was also laughable. A group called American Family Index rated us. I came out zero. Here I am, a guy who has been married to the same woman for 37 years, with five children and ten grandchildren, and I'm running against Jim Abnor, a 58-year-old bachelor who gets a 100 percent rating. I'm not against 58-year-old bachelors, not for a minute, but they are hardly a symbol of what promotes the American family."

George and Eleanor McGovern cherished their family. They loved their children as only devoted parents can. But, they were in the public eye where curiosity and attention were focused on them. They were as human as the rest of us. They experienced the joys of unusual success, the ambiguities and stresses of public life, the inevitable disappointments that come to each of us, and the bitter dregs of tragedy, but they were together to the very end.

The last two years of Eleanor's life were pain-wracked. She was tough and her will was strong, but her heart was weak and failing. During those long months George was loving-care personified. He was there for her in every possible way.

The following pages will deal with George McGovern's public career and accomplishments. Those things cannot be understood apart from his most private world.

≈

A Political Animal

JOSEPH MCGOVERN, George's father, was a minor league baseball player in the St. Louis Cardinals farm system before he became a preacher. It followed that his son George became an ardent, life-long Cardinals fan. He was a member in good standing, of the Stan Musial Society. He was a man's man (whatever that means). He was a high school athlete. As Stephen Ambrose pointed out, he was a war hero. As he grew older he jogged to stay in shape. He swam regularly in the Senate pool. He skied. He took tennis lessons, and I can tell you (from personal experience), in his 50s he could still play a mean (and I do mean, *mean*) game of tennis. But more, much more, he was a devoted family man. And, as we have already discovered, he was a political animal.

As noted earlier, after reactivating the Democratic Party in South Dakota, McGovern ran for Congress in 1956 – and he won. The outcome was not a foregone conclusion. He was challenging Harold Lovre, a four-term Congressman representing South Dakota's first congressional district. Lovre threw the book at him. He said that McGovern backed the admission of "Red China" to the United Nations and that he was a devotee of the "pinko," Henry Wallace, implying that McGovern was a communist sympathizer. McGovern responded: "I have always despised communism and every other ruthless tyranny over the mind and spirit of man." With his shoebox spilling over with 3 by 5 cards providing priceless information, and with his personable, low-key, one-on-one style of campaigning, he upset Lovre. The final count? 116,516 for McGovern; 105,835 for Lovre. George McGovern was on his way!

As a freshman congressman he was put on the House Committee on Education and Labor. His initial activities reflected his Prairie roots and loyalties. He championed higher commodity prices, grain storage programs, beef import controls, and farm price supports. "Food, farmers and his fellow man – those are the foundation stones on which George McGovern has built his philosophy of life," was an early campaign slogan. Later we will detail his immeasurable contribution to feeding the world's hungry masses. That is how he will be remembered – and rightly so. But, there was so much more.

Rather than develop a chronological trajectory of his legislative career, let's look at the themes and issues he focused on and ask the "if only" questions. (We will deal with his presidential run in a separate chapter.)

Foreign policy

George McGovern first came to national attention as a bitter, angry foe of the war in Vietnam. John Stennis was chairman of the Senate Armed Service Committee. At one point Stennis argued that American troops might have to return to Cambodia. In a rejoinder that typified his impatient anger, McGovern replied, "I'm tired of old men dreaming up wars for young men to fight. If (Stennis) wants to use American ground troops in Cambodia, let him lead the charge himself." But, the war in Southeast Asia was only one small part of the Senator's global awareness and concern.

McGovern insisted that his military policies were patterned after those of Dwight D. Eisenhower. "President Eisenhower was the single biggest influence on me in the defense field," he said. "I admire his restraint – his willingness to settle for less than total victory in Korea, his realization that money taken for defense is by its nature wasted, his willingness to undertake unilateral actions for real world security, such as restraint in nuclear testing in hopes of bringing about a test ban treaty (*The Washington Post*, 1972). He wholeheartedly agreed with Ike's concerns related to the U.S. "military-industrial complex."

The Senator took sharp issue with what he considered the short-sightedness and arrogance of George W. Bush's foreign policy. Writing for *Harper's Magazine*, he criticized its unilateralism, its rejection of the Kyoto agreement, its abrogation of the ABM Treaty, its resurrection of the Star Wars missile shield "fantasy," and its refusal to deal honestly with the United Nations and the World Court. Arguing that we should throw our full weight behind these international bodies, he wrote, "The United States has neither the right nor the ability to play the role of international policeman. The problems of the world are too great for any one nation to master."

In *Essential America*, McGovern, commenting on his world travels, insisted that America was viewed as a "bully" and a threat to world peace. He wrote, "I have yet to visit a country anywhere in the world whose rank and file citizenry supports the American invasion of Iraq, our embargo of Cuba, and our tight embrace of Israel."

Our fifty-year old embargo of Cuba was designed to bring down Fidel Castro, or at least cripple or change the direction on his government. It did none of the above. In 1963, in George McGovern's maiden speech on the Unites States Senate floor, he attacked what he called our "Castro fixation" and called for the normalization of relations. He visited Cuba many times – with Eleanor, with legislative colleagues, and with South Dakota farmers, men not known for their wild-eyed radicalism. At the very time President Bush was calling for the Cuban people to rise up against their government, McGovern, under the auspices of the Center for International Policy, was in Cuba, meeting with government officials and with Raul Castro, Fidel's brother and the acting head-of-state. McGovern, no pacifist, a war hero in his own right, was committed to diplomacy rather than truculence and violence.

Regarding the Middle East, McGovern was not an anti-Semite, nor was he a member of a Netanyahu fan club, but through his travels, studies and contacts, he had become an authority on that region. Knowing that U.S. tax-payers' money virtually subsidized the state of Israel and equipped the Israeli army, enabling it to become "a nuclear arsenal that strikes fear into its Arab neighbors," and insisting that U.S. foreign policy should not be shaped in Tel Aviv, McGovern struck a cautionary note. As President of the Middle East Policy Council (1991 to 1998), a Council praised for its even-handedness by both Colin Powell and Zbigniew Brzenzinski, McGovern urged the U.S. to be "a truly honest broker" and warned that "anything less than an even-handed approach will be rejected by the Palestinians and the Arab world, and the violence will continue."

And Iraq? George McGovern considered it Vietnam, *de-ja-vu*, all over again; not in every detail, but with frightening similarities. LBJ had his Bay of Tonkin resolution. Bush received the same sort of congressional nod. Surrounded by his neo-con brain trust, Bush manipulated erroneous, misleading, cherry-picked "intelligence," launched an unprovoked preemptive attack on Iraq, and "shocked and awed" a defenseless people into submission. Years later the carnage continued, a civil war pitting Sunni and Shia raged, and a nation was being bloodied and torn to shreds.

Writing for *The Nation* in 2002, he had "some questions for Mr. Bush," questions he had been wrestling with "both before and since September 11."

"Which course might produce better results in advancing American security?" he asked. "Is it continuing to boycott, diplomatically and commercially, such countries as Iran, Iraq, North Korea, Libya and Cuba, threatening to bomb them? Or would we be better off opening up diplomatic, travel and trade relations with these countries, including a well-staffed embassy in each? If we are fearful of a country and doubtful of its intentions, wouldn't we be safer having an embassy with professional foreign service officers located in that country to tell us what is going on?

"Our leaders frequently speak of 'rogue nations.' But what is a rogue nation? Isn't it simply one we have chosen to boycott because it doesn't always behave the way we think it should? Do such nations behave better when they are isolated and boycotted against any normal discourse? What do we have to lose in talking to 'rogue nations' diplomatically, trading with them commercially and observing their economic, political and military conditions? …

"Our military services are the best in the world. But with a military budget at record levels, do we need to allocate another $48 billion - an amount greater than the total military budget of any other nation? Is not the surest foundation for our military forces a healthy, educated, usefully employed citizenry? And is not the best way to diminish some of the international trouble spots, which might embroil our young men and women, by reducing the

43

festering poverty, misery and hopelessness of a suffering world?"

Outspoken against the war in Vietnam, McGovern was equally opposed to our Iraq fiasco. With foreign policy analyst, William Polk, he co-authored, *Out of Iraq: A Practical Way for Withdrawal Now,* calling for the immediate withdrawal of U.S. military forces from that beleaguered nation.

George McGovern may have been born and raised in a barren, isolated corner of the world. However, with the passage of time, he had developed an encyclopedic knowledge of the world, an informed conscience, a realistic view of global tensions and trouble spots, and a statesman-diplomat's ability to address complex issues, humanize them, and to deal with and move beyond them.

If only...

Domestic policy

In 1933, during the first, formative days of his administration, President Franklin D. Roosevelt gave our country the WPA (Works Progress Administration), the TVA (Tennessee Valley Authority), the AAA (the Agricultural Administration Act), the PWA (the Public Works Administration), and perhaps the most remarkable of all, the CCC (Civilian Conservation Corps). Jonathan Alter, writing about the crucial importance of those first one hundred days, said that . Roosevelt's point was plain: "Government counts, and in the right hands it can be made to work. Strong federal action, not just private voluntary action and the invisible hand of the market place, was required. ... The American people expected and deserved leadership in addressing their hardships, not just from state and local authorities but from the White House. This fundamental insight would guide politicians and would help millions of people in the years ahead" (*The Defining Moment*).

In making "a case for liberalism," George McGovern wrote, "Virtually every forward movement in our history has been a liberal initiative taken over conservative opposition: civil rights, Social Security, Medicare, rural electrification, the establishment of a minimum wage, collective bargaining, the Pure Food and Drug Act, and federal aid to education, including the land-grant colleges, to name just a few" (*Harper's Magazine*, 2001). It was obvious from the beginning that McGovern saw an activist government as a friend and not a foe.

In the summer of 1972, John Kenneth Galbraith wrote in the *Saturday Review* that "McGovern's reforms – on employment, taxes, welfare, equality – are all designed to benefit the majority. ... If one is searching for historical analogies, it could be recalled that Roosevelt's reforms of forty years ago were similarly concerned with the majority."

George McGovern was not a puppet in the hands of lobbyists and special interests; he refused to kowtoe to wealth and power. He was his own man – a man of the people called to serve the people. He saw government as an enabler, and if necessary, a provider.

If Social Security and Medicare were put up for a popular vote today, what would the outcome be? That is a no-brainer.

Contrary to Right Wing conservatives, Tea Party activists, and libertarians who have no use for government, McGovern aligned himself with our Founding Fathers and great presidents like Thomas Jefferson, Andrew Jackson, Abraham Lincoln, Teddy Roosevelt and FDR. Government was not seen as the enemy, it was an ally, a friend of the people, promoting "the general welfare."

Once again, if only…

Party reform

The 1968 Democratic Convention, featuring Mayor Daley's goon squads and Hubert Humphrey's behind-the-scenes shenanigans, brought the romanticized '60s to a screeching halt. The Old Guard had won. Humphrey gained the nomination. How could the disenchanted McCarthy/Kennedy insurgents be kept on board? For a brief moment George McGovern had stood in for the slain Robert Kennedy. He wound up supporting Humphrey. As one acceptable to both sides McGovern was named chair of a commission designed to reform the nominating process. In 1971, McGovern stepped down to run for the presidency. Committee member, Congressman Donald Fraser, was named to succeed him. In his significant study, *Quiet Revolution,* Byron Shafer credited the McGovern-Fraser Commission with "the most extensive planned change in the process of delegate selection – and hence presidential nomination – in all of American history."

In *Grassroots,* McGovern described the difference between the 1968 and the 1972 conventions. "The percentage of women in the 1972 delegation rose from 14% in 1968 to 36% in 1972; the percentage of delegates under thirty went from 2% to 23%; and blacks increased their percentage from a little over 5 to 14%." Critics charged that the reforms had empowered "hippies, women libbers, gays, kooks, and draft-dodgers." The simple fact was that smoke filled rooms, clandestine caucuses, and the old power brokers had been dethroned. The Richard Daleys, George Meanys, John Connallys and Strom Thurmonds no longer held sway. One observer wrote, "The nomination (in 1972) went to a self-proclaimed proponent of the New Politics, who defeated a captive of the Old in a stage production that at times resembled a morality play."

All of the developments were not positive. As McGovern ruefully pointed out, "When we opened the party's doors through the quota based delegate rules changes we promulgated after the 1968 convention, 20 million Democrats walked out."

The stage was set for the 1972 presidential election. What followed proved to be a national tragedy.

≈

The '72 Primaries
and Richard Nixon

IN ITS DECEMBER 27, 1971 issue, *Newsweek* magazine asked if George McGovern was "the tortoise of '72?" The answer seemed unlikely. Early on, Edmund Muskie was the prohibitive favorite, but there was a host of others in the running: Hubert Humphrey, Gene McCarthy, Henry (Scoop) Jackson, Vance Hartke, John Lindsey, Shirley Chisholm, Sam Yorty, and George Wallace. At the time Jimmie the Greek was calling Edmund Muskie a 7 to 5 favorite to defeat Nixon in November; he made George McGovern a 50 to 1 underdog to capture the nomination of his Party. National polls rated McGovern 5% in any Democratic field.

Newsweek took "the tortoise" image seriously. It spoke of McGovern's excellent organization and his army of enthusiastic young anti-war volunteers. And it spoke of his tireless, hectic, personalized style of campaigning. Citing his activities of the previous week it said, "He showed up in California for a talk at a United Auto Workers hall, a wine-tasting gala for 700 in Contra Costa County near San Francisco, a meeting at Stanford University, a fund-raising affair in Beverly Hills and a talk with black leaders in Watts. Then he flew off to Kansas City, Mo., to address the National Farmers Organization, before heading back to Washington." That is not the pace of a tortoise. But that is how McGovern campaigned in state after state, day after day.

Edmund Muskie was fading. A news magazine (*Newsweek,* 1972) reported, "There were five names on the Democratic primary election in Pennsylvania and twelve in Massachusetts on the same day...Emphatically trounced in both states, Senator Muskie removed himself from the campaign."

"One Bright Shining Moment: The Forgotten Summer of George McGovern," a prize-winning documentary featuring the voices of Howard Zinn, Gore Vidal, Dick Gregory, Gloria Steinam, and Warren Beatty, detailed McGovern's primary campaign. The *New York Daily News* called it "a riveting tale of idealism vs. cynicism." For a brief, tantalizing moment idealism won out.

In February, McGovern had written me, "The Iowa result is encouraging in the face of the Hughes endorsement, and Arizona went well, all things considered. We'll just keep rolling and doing our best. ... I think our chances are as good as anyone's at this juncture." They were - and his "best" was good enough. George McGovern, winning a cliff-hanger over Humphrey in California, gained the nomination. He would face Richard Nixon.

Richard Milhaus Nixon

Richard Nixon, the 37th president of the United States, was born in Yorba Linda, California, on January 9, 1913. He attended Fullerton High School, transferred to Whittier High School, attended Whittier College, and, graduating in 1934, he won a full scholarship to Duke University Law School in Durham, N.C. After graduating he returned to Whittier to practice law. He married a teacher, Thelma Catherine ("Pat") Ryan in 1940. They would have two daughters, Tricia and Julie.

An ambitious young man, restless in a small city, he took his family to Washington, D.C. where he got a job with the New Deal's Office of Price Administration. Disenchanted with "big government programs," he joined the Navy, serving as an aviation ground officer in the Pacific. He rose to the rank of lieutenant commander, earning two silver stars and several commendations. He resigned his commission in 1946, and returned to Whittier.

Encouraged to run for Congress, Nixon challenged a five-term liberal Democrat, Jerry Voorhees. He blamed Voorhees for harboring communist sympathies. Nixon won. As a member of the House Un-American Activities Committee he joinged others in "outing" Alger Hiss as a probable communist spy. Later he would run against Helen Gahagan Douglas for her Senate seat, charging that she was "pink right down to her underwear." He won again. He had become a well-known anti-communist. He was known, not only as, "Tricky Dick," but as "Red Hunter" as well.

He ran for governor of California and was defeated. He ran for the presidency against John F. Kennedy and was defeated. He became Dwight Eisenhower's vice-president. Then in 1968, he was elected president of the United States. That, in brief outline, is the story of Richard Nixon's life. It's an outline that offers few clues as to who the man really was – apart from his anti-communist zealotry.

Those are the bare facts, but they don't begin to tell the whole story.

Nixon's first term in the White House was marked with some significant gains in foreign policy. He relaxed tensions with the Soviet Union. With Secretary of State Kissinger by his side he opened dialogue with communist China. He promised (an utterly baseless promise) to bring an end to the war in Vietnam. Sadly, there were 25,000 more military deaths in the pitiless conflict before the war ended.

Let me get ahead of myself for a few moments. Spiro Agnew, Nixon's vice-president, resigned on October 10, 1973, disgraced after being accused of accepting bribes while serving as governor of Maryland. And Richard Nixon, threatened with impeachment, resigned on August 9, 1974.

What led to the President's downfall?

Writing forty years after Watergate, Bob Woodward and Carl Bernstein, the *Washington Post* reporters who had written *All the President's Men,* outlined the main elements of the multiple scandals and crimes that led to Nixon's forced resignation:

• "President Nixon personally approved a plan that authorized the CIA, FBI, and military-intelligence units to intensify electronic surveillance of individuals identified as 'domestic security threats.' It also allowed the interception of mail, and unauthorized break-ins by government agents of the homes of law-abiding citizens.

- "'The Nixon 'Plumbers' unit was also unleashed against perceived adversaries of the administration in an ultimately criminal fashion. Among its actions was the break-in into the headquarters of former RAND analyst Daniel Ellsberg, who had leaked the Pentagon Papers to the *New York Times*. 'You can't drop it, Bob,' Nixon instructed top aide Bob Haldeman. 'You can't let the Jew steal that stuff and get away with it. You understand?' In addition, in 1969, Henry Kissinger, President Nixon's national security advisor – and later Secretary of State – demanded that the FBI spy on 17 journalists and White House aides without court approval.

- "President Nixon's Attorney General John Mitchell approved a $250,000 criminal plan offered by G. Gordon Liddy to spy on and sabotage Democratic candidates during the 1972 election using wiretaps and burglaries, with 'at least 50 operatives – involved in the espionage and sabotage.' The chauffeur of then-leading contender, Maine Sen. Edmund Muskie, received $1000 a month to spy on the candidate and to steal campaign documents for President Nixon's campaign staff. In a memo to Haldeman and Mitchell dated April 17, 1972, White House aide, and later conservative commentator, Pat Buchanan explained, 'Our primary objective, to prevent Senator Muskie from sweeping the early primaries, locking up the convention in April, and uniting the Democratic Party behind him for the fall, has been achieved.' President Nixon also instructed his aides to order the IRS to investigate the tax returns of all potential Democratic presidential candidates.

• "President Nixon approved and directed a criminal conspiracy to try to hide his own role and that of his aides in all of the above. Six days after the Watergate break-in, Haldeman informed the president that Mitchell had suggested that the CIA be used to demand that any investigations be stopped lest they threaten 'national security.' Nixon approved it and instructed Haldeman to tell CIA Director Richard Helms to 'play it tough.' The president also instructed his aides to buy the silence of the criminals working for him. 'They have to be paid,' he said. 'That's all there is to it'" (Center for American Progress).

A number of friends and colleagues gathered to celebrate George McGovern's 85th birthday at George Washington University. There were several speakers, among them Woodward and Bernstein. In that more informal, unguarded atmosphere they spoke of Nixon's "corrupt sleaziness and Watergate's criminality," contrasting it to McGovern's "moral stature." (I was in attendance.)

In 2005, documents were released from the National Archives that underscored Nixon's lack of scruples. In 1970, U.S. forces entered Cambodia, allegedly to support the South Vietnamese. Nixon met with his aides and said they should echo that claim. "That is what we will say publicly," he explained. "Now, let's talk about what we will actually do."

As I confessed, I moved ahead of myself. But, I needed to give you a picture of the man who vanquished George McGovern in the election of 1972.

≈

Running in 'the Worst Possible Way'

IN FEBRUARY, 1972, a writer for the *National Review* said, "After 365 days on the campaign trail George McGovern has increased his popularity 300 percent, from 2 to 6 percent. The man from South Dakota, 99.4 percent liberal pure, has struck no sparks, has enlisted no legions" (*National Review*, 1972). The columnist's prediction was a tad off mark. Eight months later McGovern was running for the presidency; and run he did – only to suffer crushing defeat.

In 1973, he would say, "For many years I wanted to run for the presidency in the worst possible way – and last year I surely did."

The debacle was jump-started at 2:48 on the *morning* following his nomination. While the nation slept McGovern gave a stirring, monumental speech (some say, the best of his career), urging America to "come home". I could hardly keep my eyes open as I groggily listened. Maybe a handful of others did, but only a few thousand, according to observer analysts.

The outcome, when McGovern selected Senator Thomas Eagleton of Missouri, as his running mate, may have been sealed. Eagleton had undergone electroshock therapy. He had not told McGovern of his medical history. Eleanor had serious misgivings from the start. There was just something about Eagleton's eyes, she said, a lack of candor and a kind of dishonesty. McGovern initially stuck by his choice, "1000%" he said, but the die was cast. Eagleton met with McGovern on July 31, and they announced they had "jointly agreed that the best course (was) for Sen. Eagleton to step aside."

There followed a season of confusion. The number two slot on the ticket was offered to Humphrey, Kennedy, Muskie, and a handful of other Democratic senators. They all publicly refused. (McGovern had even called me, asking me to check out Florida's former governor, Reuben Askew).

McGovern finally asked Sargent Shriver, the former Peace Corps and anti-poverty director, to be his running-mate. The campaign limped ahead.

Valuable time had been squandered. Democrats seemed hopelessly divided. Humphrey's vicious, baseless, "amnesty, acid, and abortion" charges against McGovern, employed during the California primary, were resurrected; organized labor, with pro-war George Meany at its helm, went for Nixon; old-line party bosses like Mayor Daley, dethroned by the new party rules, stood idly by; former governor, John Connally of Texas, organized a "Democrats for Nixon" group of dissidents; and, hosts of southern Democrats, swayed by the GOP's subtly racist "southern strategy," turned their backs on McGovern. McGovern's deficit, in public opinion polls, before Humphrey began his assault in the California primary, was 10 points. At the end of the Eagleton-Shriver nightmare, it had dropped to 34 points.

McGOVERN AND NIXON were polar opposites. The Rev. Charles P. Henderson, Jr., a chaplain at Princeton, wrote a book called, *The Nixon Theology*. He decided to write the book as he observed the student protests related to U.S. troop movements into Cambodia. "At Princeton," he explained, "the anti-war sentiment had the tone of 'moral outrage instead of political analysis of Nixon political policy'.

Outcries against the administration's Cambodia 'incursion' were followed by President Nixon's appearance at a Billy Graham Crusade in Knoxville, Tennessee, where the chief executive was warmly welcomed." ("Nixon and McGovern stances on theology, morals probed" (*The Texas Methodist,* 1972). More on the Nixon-Graham bond will follow.

A revealing sidebar:

Busing of students to public schools was being employed by authorities to defeat segregation in 1972. George McGovern was speaking to 3000 students jammed into an auditorium at the University of Illinois. President Nixon was scheduled to speak at 9 o'clock. McGovern thought everyone should hear the president. A television set was brought on stage, a microphone was held up to it, and the students heard the president deliver a strident anti-busing tirade. The columnist, Anthony Lewis, described what followed:

"When the President was finished, Senator McGovern switched off the set and went to the rostrum. 'What we have just witnessed', he said, 'is a collapse of moral and political leadership by the President: a total surrender to Wallaceism and the demagoguery it represents...' For perhaps five or ten minutes McGovern spoke about the issues posed by the Nixon address. The response in that hall was electric. Of course, it was a sympathetic audience, but even the most detached observers were impressed by what McGovern was doing – his passion, his articulation, his courage."

In September of '72, Charles Henderson, the Princeton chaplain, wrote an article for *Commonweal*, titled, "The (Social) Gospel according to (1) Richard Nixon (2) George McGovern" (*Commonweal*, 1972). In it he said, "McGovern shares the President's conviction that work is a virtue, *per se*.....Where Nixon places the moral responsibility upon the individual to find a job, regardless of the circumstances, McGovern places the moral responsibility upon government to guarantee a living wage to every citizen, regardless of merit." McGovern called his approach, "a kind of intelligent, modern approach to the puritan ethic. It's saying that we shouldn't waste labor, we shouldn't waste human life."

In the same article, Henderson wrote, "Today McGovern's closest contact in the hierarchy of his denomination is Bishop James Armstrong. Since 1963, when McGovern met Armstrong in Uppsala (actually, it was 1968), the two have become close associates and friends. They confer almost weekly, discussing issues of mutual concern. I asked the Bishop to describe the content of those conversations. 'They involve littler theology in the abstract sense,' he said, 'but deal with ethical and social issues in a political context.'"

Comparing Nixon and McGovern, the chaplain wrote, "There is an unmistakable pattern in the President's ethics; he identifies his Protestant convictions almost exclusively with a rugged individualism, he ignores the social causes of our ills...McGovern, by contrast, is concerned chiefly about the public responsibility for larger social injustices. He sees our sins in a collective sense, and is prepared to offer a more comprehensive solution."

Where Richard Nixon appeared to thrive on moving from crisis to crisis (many of them self-induced), McGovern was steady, conscientious and consistent. James David Barber said it like this: "If McGovern's life is a prevailing wind, Nixon's is stormy weather" (*Saturday Review*, 1972).

The campaign role of the Religious

Although the Nixons rarely attended church before he was elected President, that image of relative indifference had to change. During his first administration, President Nixon initiated religious services conducted in the East Room of the White House. It was more convenient than attending a regular church, and he could hand-pick both the preachers and those who would be in attendance.

Nixon had appeared at a Billy Graham Crusade in Knoxville. That was not unusual. Cecil Boswell, in his *Prince of War: Billy Graham's Crusade for a Wholly Christian Empire,* wrote, "During the 1972 campaign, Graham worked unabashedly for Nixon's reelection, albeit behind the scenes."

Graham had sent Nixon a hand-written note in December, 1970, saying, "My expectations were high when you took office nearly two years ago, but you have exceeded them in every way! You have given moral and spiritual leadership to the nation at a time when we desperately need it – in addition to courageous political leadership! Thank you!"

George Wallace, the Democratic antithesis of everything McGovern stood for, had been shot and critically wounded in May. Paralyzed, a paraplegic, he remained a factor in the '72 campaign. White House operatives feared that, in spite of being wheel-chair bound, he might try to run. They asked Billy Graham to lend them a hand. Graham had access to Wallace through Wallace's wife, Cornelia, who had recently become a Christian. Graham agreed to help. On July 18, he reached Wallace by phone and the next day he reported to Nixon that Wallace had assured him that there was no way he would turn a hand to help McGovern, assured him that he would not run, and told him that three out of four Wallace voters would support the President. Billy Graham had become a political operative.

The White House was afraid that McGovern might be seen as "the religious candidate" in the race. In *Billy, You Stay Out of Politics,* the author reported that Graham "was particularly concerned about the Religious Leaders for McGovern group. Organized by Methodist Bishop James Armstrong and consisting of over two hundred liberal religious leaders, the group had set out to correct what its members believed to be Republican misstatements about McGovern. Graham both liked and admired Armstrong and feared the movement might have considerable impact." Would Graham be willing to help establish a counter-organization? He decided against that, but "quasi endorsed" Nixon by announcing to the Associated Press that he expected Nixon to carry every state in the union with the probable exception of South Dakota. He told the *Charlotte Observer* that Nixon would "go down in history as the greatest President because he studied, prepared himself, disciplined himself for the Presidency, and the effects show now."

It should be noted that after the Nixon tapes were released, spilling over with obscenities and anti-Semitism, Billy Graham distanced himself from the disgraced president and sought out George McGovern to apologize to him.

Interestingly, in 2012, Graham told Mitt Romney he would "do all (he) could to help him" in his run against Barack Obama in the presidential race of 2012. Graham was in his 90's. His son, Franklin, explaining his father's stance said, "He cannot vote for a candidate who supports same sex marriage and advocates abortion" (*Christian Century,* 2012). Obama did support women's abortion rights and believed in the right of same-sex couples to marry – and the old evangelist did continue to be a political player.

About Religious Leaders for McGovern – it included among its members some of the outstanding religious luminaries of the 20th century. They were: John C. Bennett, President Emeritus of Union Theological Seminary in New York; William Sloan Coffin, the widely known anti-war chaplain at Yale; Harvey Cox, the popular, outspoken Harvard Professor of Divinity; Robert McAfee Brown, Stanford University's proponent of liberation theology; Georgia Harkness, Professor Emeritus, Pacific School of Religion; David Colwell, Moderator of the United Church of Christ; Rabbi Abraham Heschel of Jewish Theological Seminary in New York; Bishop Brooke Moseley, President of Union Theological Seminary; Krister Stendahl, Dean of the Harvard Divinity School; Sister Mary Luke Tobin, a Roman Catholic ecumenical leader; and a number of United Methodist bishops.

They all wrote glowingly of George McGovern. Robert McAfee Brown's words were typical: "I am endorsing Senator McGovern because it seems to me that the times call for forthrightness and directness and courage in the White House and that Senator McGovern has been displaying these qualities to a degree that puts him far ahead of any other aspirants for this high office. He has been willing to take 'controversial' stands, to espouse causes long before they were popular, and to give a kind of moral and political leadership that our country desperately needs. He brings a combination of moral commitment and political expertise to the concerns of the Presidency at a time when both of those qualities are particularly needed on the national scene."

On election eve I presented "the case for McGovern" in *The Christian Century* (November 1, 1972). I said, "President Nixon has gone to Peking and Moscow. According to the TV blurbs advocating his reelection, these are his major accomplishments in office. I quite agree. But the irony is that Richard Nixon was one of the major architects of the cold war. In contrast, George McGovern was calling for the recognition of the Peoples' Republic of China in the mid-1950s. What was Mr. Nixon saying on that subject then?" I added, "I know George McGovern. He is a strong and good man. If he becomes President he will usher in a new era of decency, self-respect and hope for the American people.

The Christian Century, mainstream Protestantism's most influential journalistic voice, endorsed McGovern.

The Roman Catholic, *Commonweal* endorsed him, saying, "The editors of *Commonweal* formally endorse George McGovern for President of the United States. This is no routine decision. Only once in our almost half century of publishing have we backed a candidate: Adlai E. Stevenson in 1952. In the past, even in 1928 and 1960 – elections which in a symbolic sense, specifically concerned Catholics – we have restricted our editorial discussion to the issues. (This election) may be a turning point in American history, a year when political, economic and cultural patterns are set that will determine the future nature of the American character. The real America is being asked to stand up."

Well, America stood up – but not very tall. The final vote count?

Richard Nixon:	46,740,323
George McGovern:	28,901,598

What a travesty! If only the numbers had been reversed.

If only!

≈

The Aftermath

SPEAKING IN AMES, IOWA, in 1975, George McGovern shouldered the blame for his defeat in '72. It resulted, he said, from his failure to adequately explain the issues, from his staff's disorganization and disputes, and from his "most serious error," his selection of Tom Eagleton as his running-mate (*Washington Post*, 1975). The fact is - his self-criticism, partially true as it may have been, was far from enough to explain the enormity of his defeat.

There were any number of factors: the unprecedented criminality of McGovern's foe, the occasional ineptness of McGovern's staff,

McGovern's lack of charisma as a campaigner, the failure of the American people to understand the tragic dimensions of the war in Southeast Asia, the refusal of the smoke-filled-room party bosses of organized labor and the traditional Democratic "establishment" to back him, the media's failure to take Watergate seriously and its inclination to draw a caricature of McGovern as "the Prairie Preacher," (see: "George McGovern, Prairie Preacher," James Jackson Kilpatrick, *National Review,* February 18, 1972) and, the laziness and failure of the U.S. electorate to do its homework and learn about the candidates and the issues

MCGOVERN WAS A RESILIENT MAN. A few days after the election he sent me a note. "Although we were disappointed in the results," he wrote, "I do feel that our campaign has made a contribution to the public and political life of this country. Perhaps, too, we may have chartered a course on the issues that others will follow in the future." He continued, "I am going to do everything I can in the coming months for South Dakota and our nation. ... A good deal of my effort, of course, will be directed toward seeking re-election to the Senate in 1974."

That all sounded thoughtfully reflective, but the McGoverns' reactions ran deeper than that; far deeper. They were crushed.

Depressed, Eleanor even more than George, they flew to London. They briefly considered moving to England.

On January 20, 1973, Richard Nixon was inaugurated. A few hours later McGovern, still in England, addressed an audience at the Oxford Union and spoke of the abuses of the Nixon presidency. Many considered it ill-timed and ill-mannered. Realizing that he had to get over his "bitterness and self-pity," he turned a page and resumed his public career.

In 1974, McGovern faced a formidable challenger for his Senate seat. Lt. Col. Leo Thorsness, an Air Force pilot, had been downed over North Vietnam and had earned the Medal of Honor. He was repatriated after suffering through six years of incarceration as a prisoner of war in a North Vietnamese prison camp, and was determined to unseat the incumbent Senator. He argued that McGovern had been giving aid and comfort to the communists while he was rotting in a North Vietnamese prison as a POW.

Interestingly enough, the war did not prove to be a decisive issue. Just two weeks before the election (October 14, 1974), the *Aberdeen American News* called the race a toss-up. The paper reported that "both candidates agree the major issues in the farm state are inflation, taxes and instability of farm prices." Thorsness projected the image of "a man with a mission." The mission was aborted. McGovern won 53% of the vote.

I had been dabbling in politics since George Smathers had run his racist campaign for the Senate against Claude Pepper in Florida in 1950. I had been a member of the Platform Committee, and vice-chair of Hoosiers for a Democratic Alternative (to LBJ) in Indiana during the presidential contest of 1968. I had organized Religious Leaders for McGovern in '72. However, nothing approached my involvement in George McGovern's bid for re-election in 1974.

I gave the keynote address at South Dakota's Democratic state convention. I prayed at Jefferson-Jackson day dinners all over the place. I was seen on statewide television urging the re-election of the Senator. I even flew with Eleanor to a Hutterite-Mennonite Centennial Celebration in Freeman, a town in the southern part of the state, to put in a good word for my friend, George. The straw that broke the camel's back, however, was a letter I posted to the editors of the state's newspapers (along with copies of McGovern's '72 campaign speeches), asking them to help correct the misrepresentations that had plagued McGovern's bid for the White House two years earlier.

Harold Jones, editor of the *Redfield Press,* took sharp issue with my right to do so. The state's leading newspaper, the *Sioux Falls Argus Leader,* headlined: "Editor chides bishop for McGovern letter" (August 28, 1974).The state's media followed the controversy. The *Des Moines* (Iowa) *Register* editorialized:

"Throughout recorded history people have looked to religious leaders for moral direction and assurance. The purview of the Hebrew prophets and early Christian evangelists, the papacy and the Protestant reformers, were not restricted by artificial barriers separating the sacred from the secular ... Bishop Armstrong's critics, by trying to silence him on matters touching political issues, want to erect a wall far higher than anything envisioned in 1791."

It also said:

"While the bishop was in Europe last month, the largest church in his jurisdiction, First United Methodist Church at Sioux Falls, S.D., adopted a resolution requesting him to 'refrain from political and other secular affairs outside the normal patterns of church behavior.'"

Actually, "the church" had not adopted the resolution. A number of lay members of the church met and adopted the resolution; 125 voting for it and 53 opposing it. The church had nearly 3000 members.

In follow-up articles the *Argus Leader* reported that the resolution had been engineered by Thorsness supporters. I had been attending a world peace conference in Belgium when the people met in Sioux Falls. After returning from Europe I drove to Sioux Falls and met with about 300 members and friends of the church in the sanctuary of the church. I read a rather lengthy statement, expressing my regrets, saying, "If I have embarrassed anyone I am truly sorry." I said, "Let us deal with the issue at hand, the role of the clergy in public life as well as the individual clergyman's participation in political and secular affairs." There ensued a lively discussion, punctuated by both boos and cheering. The following day the *Argus Leader* featured a three-column, blow-by-blow, description of the event, headlined: "Spirit of Reconciliation Emerges from Meeting of Bishop Armstrong, Methodist Church Critics."

Larry Pressler, a young Republican candidate for Congress, wrote me a letter of strong support.

Senator McGovern, who had been following the fray, wrote me a warm letter of appreciation, and confirmed that Jerry Simmons, who had spearheaded the assault on me, was a long-time foe, and an ardent supporter of Thorsness.

Thorsness had been defeated. McGovern returned to the Senate.

The movie, "All the President's Men," dealt with its subject in detail. Then, with the sound of clattering typewriters, it announced Nixon's defeat and came to an abrupt end. That's what I'm about to do.

McGovern resumed his senatorial duties until 1980. In 1980, along with Frank Church of Idaho, Birch Bayh of Indiana, Warren Magneson of Washington, and Gaylord Nelson of Wisconsin, all liberal Democrats, George McGovern was defeated, and the "Reagan revolution" claimed its first victims. That same year a young, one-term Congressman from Indiana, Dan Quayle, was elected to the Senate.

George McGovern's primary claim to fame, however, should not be overlooked.

≈

'Give Us This Day
Our Daily Bread'

"HUNGER IS THE #1 HEALTH THREAT in the world today, killing more people than AIDS, malaria and tuberculosis combined. Over 850 million people – or 1 in 7 people on earth – suffer from hunger. There are 350 million hungry children in the world, a level more than the entire population of the United States. Every day, 25,000 people die of hunger. Every four seconds someone, somewhere, dies of hunger. Yet, hunger is a solvable problem. There is enough food in the world to provide every man, woman and child with enough to eat. The challenge is getting food to those who need it most."

These words, taken from a "Friends of the World Food Program" brochure, summarize one of humankind's most urgent challenges.

George McGovern will be remembered for many things – for being a friend and ally of the American farmer, for opposing a senseless war in Southeast Asia, for being "the most decent man in the U.S. Senate," for being the "Prairie Statesman" from South Dakota. But, above all else, he will be remembered as a man who authored programs that fed hungry people around the world. In 1962, McGovern had an audience with Pope John XXIII. Addressing the Senator, the Pope said, "When you meet your Maker, and he asks, 'Have you fed the hungry and given drink to the thirsty and cared for the lonely,' you can answer. 'Yes.'" What led to such praise? In the words of the poet, "Let me count the ways."

In 1961, President John F. Kennedy named McGovern, Director of the Food for Peace program. Kennedy had said, "Food is strength and food is peace and food is freedom and food is helping people around the world whose good will and friendship we want." Apart from its humanitarian dimensions it was seen as an important tool, every bit as important as military arms, in our fight against communism during the Cold War.

The Food for Peace Program was initiated by President Eisenhower, but McGovern hit the ground running and vigorously expanded it. In 1964, he wrote his first book, *War Against Want: America's Food for Peace Program.* It is estimated that since the inception of the program more than 3 billion people in 150 countries have benefited from its food assistance.

From 1968 to 1977, McGovern chaired the Senate's Committee on Nutrition and Human Needs. That committee was responsible for most of the food legislation enacted during that significant decade.

From 1998 to 2001, McGovern served as American Ambassador to the United Nations Food and Agriculture Agencies. In September of 2000, he sent me a postcard from Rome where his offices were located. He wrote, "My current passion is to get the U.N. committed to providing a school lunch every day for every school age child in the world. I persuaded Clinton to start us this academic year with the first $300 million. I'm hard at work here persuading other countries to join us. Britain and Canada are on board. If we can pull this off it may be the most important victory of my life."

The *Sioux Falls Argus Leader*, reporting McGovern's reappointment to his U.N. post by President Bush, wrote, "George McGovern says putting food in the bellies of 300 million hungry children worldwide is the most important challenge of his long life of public service ... More important than his push to end the war in Vietnam, more important than his 1972 failed bid to win the presidency."

In 2000, McGovern had talked President Bill Clinton into establishing the Global Food for Education Initiative. During 2001 and 2002, the program fed 7 million children in 38 countries.

In August 2000, President Clinton awarded McGovern the Presidential Medal of Freedom, the highest honor an American civilian can receive. At that time he said, "George McGovern is one of the greatest humanitarians of our time, and the world will benefit from his legacy for generations to come."

In 2001, McGovern's book, *The Third Freedom: Ending Hunger in Our Time,* was published. It proposed a program that would eliminate hunger within thirty years.

In 2002, the U.S. Congress established the George McGovern-Robert Dole International Food for Education and Child Nutrition Program. According to Friends of the World Food Program, the food provided for malnourished children in the world's poorest countries. "These school meals...ensure that these children receive at least one nutritious meal a day. These meals relieve short-term hunger and increase children's capacity to learn. Where school feeding programs are offered, enrollment and attendance rates increase significantly, especially for girls."

McGovern was once asked whether the war against hunger should start at home before going abroad. McGovern replied, "Why not do both? There are, after all, enough resources in the world to reach all hungry people. Why give any quarter in the war against hunger?" He certainly did not (Lambers, 2012).

In 2006, it is estimated that nearly 27 million Americans were receiving food stamps; 30 million youngsters were having their school lunches provided; nearly 10 million were receiving school breakfasts; and, the McGovern-Dole International School Nutrition Program was feeding 3,400,000 children in 15 countries.

On October 16, 2008, George McGovern and Robert Dole were made World Food Prize laureates for their efforts to alleviate world hunger. Special mention was made of the school lunch programs that improved the health and hopes of vast numbers of children.

World Food Program director, Ertharin Cousin, says, "George McGovern saw – way before anyone else – how the simple sustained act of putting a meal in the hands of a poor child could change that child's life and give them a chance for a better future."

McGovern once said, "Hunger is the silent enemy. It is a thief in the night that steals away the children in 10,000 villages around the globe." He, more than anyone of his time, had recognized the ominous importance of that thief in the night.

≈

A Unique Legacy

AFTER HIS DEFEAT IN 1980, George McGovern did not sit idly by. Opposing our war in Iraq, he likened it to our ill-fated Vietnam misadventure. He co-authored a book about the war's futility and a responsible way out. In 1981 he founded Americans for Common Sense, an organization designed to combat Jerry Falwell's Moral Majority and the growing influence of the Religious Right. He served as a visiting professor at Columbia University, Cornell University, American University, and even the University of Berlin in Germany. He replaced Stephen Ambrose, author of *The Wild Blue,* as a professor at the University of New Orleans, for a time.

President Gerald Ford named him a United Nations delegate to the General Assembly, and President Jimmie Carter named him U.N. delegate for the Special Section on Disarmament. (McGovern confessed later to Larry King that in 1976, he had voted for Ford, a known and respected public servant, who was challenged by Carter, a relatively unknown quantity at the time. He did vote for Carter in the next election – to no avail.)

McGovern served as president of the Middle East Policy Council from 1991 to 1998.

An honorary life member of the board of Friends of the World Food Program, McGovern was appointed as the first U.S. Ambassador on World Hunger by WFP. Feeding the hungry remained his #1 priority. He once said, "After I'm gone I want people to say about me: he did the best he could to end hunger in this country and the world."

Don Messer, who served as Dakota Wesleyan's president, later as president of the Iliff School of Theology, and today as executive director of a global AIDs ministry, had been a close friend of McGovern for forty years. He wrote, "Faith and action were very closely related to him. A man of really deep faith, his passion and energy have caused worldwide good. His work to end world hunger speaks volumes... Other politicians when they leave office grab lucrative lobbyist positions, but McGovern devoted his life to ways of ending hunger in the world."

In January 2008, McGovern wrote an op-ed piece for the *Washington Post* calling for the impeachment of President Bush and Vice-President Cheney, insisting that they had violated the Constitution, transgressed international law, and repeatedly lied to the American people as they led us into Iraq. The article's sub title was, "Nixon Was Bad. These Guys are Worse." McGovern simply refused to lay down his arms. He was a warrior, enlisted in causes of humanitarian righteousness, until he drew his last breath.

The former Senator aged. He grew frail; his health was failing. In 2011, he was treated for exhaustion. Later that year he was hospitalized after a serious fall. He was hospitalized again in April, 2012, due to fainting spells.

On the morning of October 21, 2012, surrounded by his family and a few friends, George McGovern died in a Sioux Falls hospice care center.

President Obama said. "George McGovern dedicated his life to serving the country he loved... When the people of South Dakota sent him to Washington, this hero of war became a champion for peace. After his career in Congress, he became a leading voice in the fight against hunger. George was a statesman of great conscience and conviction, and Michelle and I share our thoughts and prayers with his family."

Joe Biden, who had been an early admirer and disciple, and who spoke at the prayer service in Sioux Falls the night before McGovern's funeral, said, "Jill and I are profoundly saddened. ... I was honored to serve with him, to know him, and to call him a friend. George believed deeply in public service. It defined him as a senator and as a man."

Bill and Hillary Clinton responded: "We first met George while campaigning for him in 1972. Our friendship endured for forty years. ... George always worked to advance the common good and help others realize their potential. Of all his passions he was most dedicated to feeding the hungry, at home and around the world."

George McGovern's funeral service was held at the Washington Pavilion of Arts and Science in Sioux Falls. Joe Biden, Walter Mondale, John Kerry and Gary Hart, joined the mourners. Vice-President Biden was one of those who spoke at the Prayer Service at the First United Methodist Church the night before the funeral. There were several United Methodist ministers on the platform. Years earlier, as their bishop, I had ordained each of them. One of them, Bishop Bruce Ough, the current United Methodist bishop in South Dakota, delivered a moving, heartfelt sermon at the funeral. Among many other things he said:

'South Dakota has lost one of its beloved sons of the prairie. Our nation has lost one of its true heroes and patriots and an unwavering clarion voice for peace, justice, compassion and decency. The world community has lost a champion and friend of the poor and hungry. The People of Faith have lost a mature disciple of the Gospel of Jesus and a follower of the Methodist way of life – to do no harm, to do good, and to stay in love with God."

The McGovern legacy

Celebrating a Legacy is the title of a glossy, tasteful booklet that was distributed when the magnificent George and Eleanor McGovern Library and Center for Public Service, located in the heart of the Dakota Wesleyan University campus, was dedicated in September of 2006. Appropriately illustrated, it tells the story of the McGoverns from infancy on. It describes their childhoods, their educations, their life together, his service in World War II, his life as a college professor, a successful politician, and as a uniquely influential citizen of the world.

Robert Duffett, President of DWU at the time, speaking at the dedication of the McGovern Center, said, "In celebrating the accomplishments of the McGoverns and the Wesleyan tradition of developing visionary leaders, we are also creating a lasting tribute to the impact of higher education, the importance of leadership and social concern, and the vital integration of service into every aspect of life." In the university that meant so much to McGovern, higher education and public service were firmly intertwined.

The blended qualities of humility, grace, dedication, hard work, uncanny vision, progressive idealism, hard-nosed realism, courage and bold action were remarkably fused in the character and personality of George Stanley McGovern. A consensus emerges from those who witnessed and shared McGovern's public life, a consensus confirmed by my own observation and experience. George McGovern's legacy might well be defined by the following qualities:

- **human decency** – acknowledged by all who knew him.
- **loyalty** – to family, friends, and the underdog who needed him most.
- **truthfulness** – he said the first law of politics is, "Don't lie."

- **progressive idealism** – a description of his public career.
- **principled patriotism** – demonstrated over the long years of his public life.
- **informed compassion** – for the hungry, wayward, and broken.
- **forgiveness** – he had no "enemies list."
- **leadership** – underscored by Stephen Ambrose in *The Wild Blue.*
- **humility** – sinful pride was absent.
- **healthy ambition** – his upward drive was always under control; and
- **warmhearted humanity** – it's simply who he was.

Compare these qualities to what Frank Bruni called the "freak show" of recent garish political behavior: Mark Sanford and his Argentine girl friend, Elliot Spitzer and his high priced call-girls, Anthony Wiener and his weird fascination with his own anatomy, and San Diego Mayor Bob Filmer with his groping hands and boorish behavior. These sad cartoon characters seem far removed from the Prairie Statesman from South Dakota and all he represented.

The George McGovern I have described is not a myth. He was a flesh-and-blood, here-and-now, occasionally flawed, but always with his "eyes on the prize" human being; a mortal who became a selfless servant of and for the human family.

If only, *if only*, the presidential election of 1972 had turned out differently, the story of our land would be a far different, far better and far healthier, story.

If only ...

≈

WORKS CITED

The Seedbed of Values
"Notes of a Preacher's Kid," *The Christian Ministry*, July, 1971

Eleanor and Patriotism
Robert Sam Anson, *McGovern*, p. 160
Time Magazine, August 7, 1972
"The Higher Patriotism," *Response*, September, 1971
"Letter from Birmingham Jail," Martin Luther King, Jr.
"The New Patriotism," *Nation Building*, May 23, 1991
The Nation, April 11, 2005

Society and the History Prof
Dorothy Schweider

Nancy Grund
Grassroots, p. 31
Carl Rogers, *A Way of Being*, p. 350

A Political Animal
"McGovern on Defense: A Disciple of Eisenhower," *The Washington Post*, June 25, 1972
The Nation, April 22, 2002
Jonathan Alter, *The Defining Moment*
"The Case for Liberalism," *Harper's Magazine*, Dec., 2001
Saturday Review, July 1, 1972

The '72 Primaries and Richard Nixon
Newsweek, May 8, 1972
"Worse Than Watergate," Center for American Progress

Running in "the Worst Possible Way"
James Jackson Kilpatrick, "George McGovern, Prairie Preacher," *National Review*, February 18, 1972
"Nixon and McGovern stances on theology, morals probed," *The Texas Methodist*, August 11, 1972
"The Social Gospel According to (1) Richard Nixon (2) George McGovern." *Commonweal,* September 29, 1972
"The Question of Presidential Character," *Saturday Review*, September 23, 1972
The Christian Century, November 14, 2012
Commonweal, October 15, 1972

The Aftermath
Washington Post, October 26, 1975
James Jackson Kilpatrick, "George McGovern, Prairie Preacher," *National Review*, February, 1972
Aberdeen American News, October 14, 1974
Sioux Falls Argus Leader, August 28, 1974

"Give Us This Day Our Daily Bread"

"George McGovern Championed Food for Peace," Willian Lambers, October 31, 2012

≈

ABOUT THE AUTHOR

DR. JAMES ARMSTRONG is a professor of Ethics and Philosophy at Rollins College in Winter Park, Florida. He is a retired Christian minister with a graduate studies background in psychotherapy and decades of practice as a professional counselor. He and George McGovern were longtime personal friends. In the "Foreword" to Dr. Armstrong's book, *Living and Dying with Purpose and Grace* (Rider Green Book Publishers, 2010), the former U.S. Senator wrote the following:

"I first heard Jim Armstrong more than forty years ago and believe he has been one of the most effective preachers of our time. His fluency and power have been a joy and inspiration to me and to thousands of others. The Roman, Quintilian, once defined rhetoric as 'a good man speaking well.' The words that follow reveal a good man thinking and writing well, and in the process, the author has provided a helping hand to all of us."

≈

ADDITIONAL COPIES of this book can be ordered on Amazon.com. To inquire about discounts for volume orders (five or more copies), please contact **info@psaofmaine.com** or call (207) 457-5088.

Made in the USA
Charleston, SC
16 July 2014